Photography

An Illustrated
Teach Yourself book

if you have two hands, one eye, imagination and a decent camera you can be a good photographer . . .

Ronald Spillman
A.I.I.P.

Illustrated Teach Yourself Photography

KNIGHT BOOKS
Hodder & Stoughton

ISBN 0 304 19607 6

Copyright © 1969, 1975 Hodder and Stoughton Limited

First published 1969 by Brockhampton Press
(now Hodder and Stoughton Children's Books,) Salisbury Road, Leicester

This edition published 1975 by Knight Books, the paperback division of
Hodder and Stoughton Children's Books, Salisbury Road, Leicester.

Printed in Great Britain by Fletcher & Son Limited, Norwich,
and bound by Richard Clay (The Chaucer Press) Ltd, Bungay, Suffolk.

Contents

METRIC MEASUREMENTS

The following approximate equivalents
may help you:

10.2cm = 4 inches
12.7cm = 5 inches
17.8cm = 7 inches
30.5cm = 12 inches
40.6cm = 16 inches
50.8cm = 20 inches

0.9m   = 3 feet
1.5m   = 5 feet
2.1m   = 7 feet
3.7m   = 12 feet
15m   = 50 feet
457.2m = 500 yards

28.4ml = 1 fluid ounce
568ml = 20 fluid ounces

Foreword

Exciting changes are taking place in photography, not
only on the technical side, for technically superb
photographs were being made thirty years ago, but also in
the new sophistication of the medium.

A groundwork of the 'know-how' of photography is
still required, though technical developments have
removed much of the laboriousness from the act of taking
photographs. A whole new generation of young men and
women, freed from technical slavery, has learned that the
most important part of the camera is the eye that is put to
the viewfinder. And they have learned to *see*. The
'symbols' of modern photography, i.e. light and shade,
form, sharpness and blur, colour mood, are being used by
today's photographers to describe graphically their
reactions to the tragic, the beautiful, the humorous, and
the commonplace.

It has been estimated that four-fifths of the film exposed
in this country is used by the 'occasional' cameraman to
record holidays and happy moments. The technical
advances of which I have spoken have made even these
holiday snaps of better quality. More and more of today's
amateurs, though, are becoming less and less satisfied
with the traditional forms of amateur photography. Farm-
yards seen through wagon wheels, windmills against the
sky, and portraits entitled *Pensive* (usually sister or girl-
friend feeling a bit ridiculous under a shawl), are still
winning prizes all over the country – just as identical
prints did twenty, thirty, and forty years ago.

But the wind of change is ruffling even the greybeards
at the camera clubs. Live action portraits taken in daylight,
genuine expressions of personality, landscapes which say
something about environment and change; truthful
photographic comments on the tragi-comedy of life; these
things can no longer be dismissed as *avant-garde*, or way
out. This is the new photography.

Advertisements in photographic magazines try to make

the newcomer believe that only with a large, expensive outfit will he be able to produce good pictures. This is rubbish, though very profitable to the advertisers. A thousand pounds' worth of equipment used by an unimaginative, technical expert, will produce technically perfect photographs which are not worth looking at. On the other hand, a photographer with a fresh, imaginative eye will produce good pictures on a camera costing ten pounds.

Notice that I differentiate between photographs and pictures. A photograph, however correctly focused, exposed and processed, will be a mere technical record unless the subject is seen artistically.

My object, therefore, is twofold. To teach the reader how to select and use his equipment correctly, and how to produce pictures rather than mere photographs.

Whether your ultimate aim is the album, the exhibition wall, or publication, thoughtful study of this book will certainly put you squarely on the right road to success.

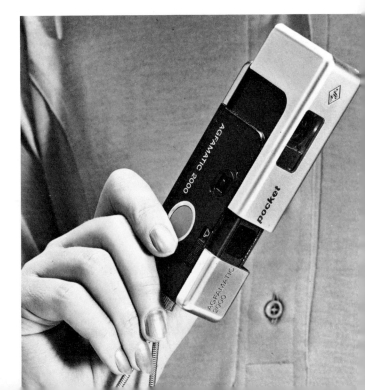

110 is the newest size, introduced by Kodak. Tiny negatives on new Kodacolor 11 film give good enlargements up to about 10.2 × 15.2cm. Agfa have also introduced improved film for this size. This is the Agfamatic 2000.

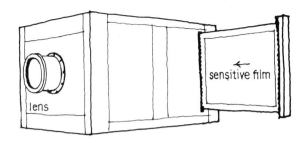

1. The equipment for the job

Basically, a camera is a light-tight box with a film at one end and a lens at the other. It is the purpose of the lens to project an image of the scene before it on to the film. The very early cameras seen in museums are simply the basic instrument here described.

The film surface contains a layer of light-sensitive silver halides which undergoes a chemical change on exposure to light. As the picture projected on to the film by the lens is composed of light-rays, therefore it is this picture that records itself on the sensitive surface of the film.

But unfortunately we cannot just point such a box at whatever interests us, and produce a good, sharp picture. There are two further basic requirements. First, the picture projected by the lens must be correctly focused, and sharp. Second, we must estimate and control the period of time for which the light picture is allowed to affect the film.

Therefore:

(1) The lens must be of good optical quality, and provided with a means by which it can be focused.

(2) A shutter is necessary, allowing us to select a suitable length of exposure or 'speed' for any given lighting conditions.

The complicated progress from the original, simple box to the highly sophisticated modern camera, smothered in gadgets, is due almost entirely to the efforts of designers to meet these two basic requirements.

Possibly, if your future path in photography is in one of the professional fields, you will require a fair amount of specialized equipment. On the other hand, if you will be content to produce superb pictures of 'faces and places', a simple instrument costing ten pounds or so may suit you admirably. That, and careful study of these chapters.

A hundred years ago the intending purchaser of a camera looked at the beautifully dovetailed woodwork, and ducked his head under a dark cloth to examine the image cast by the lens on a ground-glass screen, to make up his mind whether this was 'his' camera.

Today, the novice is confronted by a bewildering array of specifications, all of which, he is assured, are *New!* and the *Latest*, and without which he cannot possibly be 'with it', in the photographic sense.

There follows a short glossary of the more usual specifications used by manufacturers and salesmen. Read them through and decide which are relevant to your purpose. Many will be an unnecessary encumbrance in simpler kinds of picture-making. Bear in mind that the prime essential is a good lens, and a camera that is equipped with this is unlikely to be shoddy in any other respect.

Also, bear in mind that manufacturers of cameras in the middle price bracket (£20 to £75) are faced with great pressure from competitors, which often forces them to work 'down to a price', while still offering more gadgets than the opposition. Thus, it follows that a camera of modest specification may be a better instrument than a similarly-priced one with a vast list of specifications.

Aberrations

The correction of faults accounts for most of the cost of a good lens. Common aberrations are coma, astigmatism, and pincushion and barrel distortion. Coma causes the image of a point off the central axis to appear as a comet-shaped fuzz. Astigmatism is an oblique aberration affecting only the margins of the field. In barrel distortion straight lines tend to bow outwards (convex). In pincushion distortion straight lines tend to bow inwards (concave). Barrel distortion is particularly difficult to correct in wide-angle lenses, where acute perspective is often introduced.

Anastigmat

Most modern lenses are anastigmats, that is, they have been corrected from astigmatism, or distortion of focus. A good anastigmat will also have been corrected from other faults found in less complex lenses.

Bellows

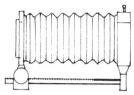

On many cameras a special bellows close-focusing device may be inserted between lens and camera body, making photography possible at extremely close range. On older small cameras, and on modern technical cameras, integral bellows are used in conjunction with some form of rack-and-pinion focusing. Smaller cameras usually have helical focusing.

Cassette

emulsion

The small, light-tight container in which 35mm film may be bought. Some expensive miniatures (Leica) have reloadable cassettes. These must be loaded in the dark-room, but enable one to save money by using 'reloads' and bulk film.

Coating

A microscopic film of fluoride applied to each of the air/ glass surfaces of a lens. It serves two purposes. First, it eliminates light-loss from reflection, most important in lenses containing a large number of elements. Second, and because of this, it gives a clearer image, especially in against-the-light photography. Also known as 'blooming', thus, a coated or bloomed lens.

Compur shutter

(Also known as compound, front-lens, or leaf shutter.) Normally, a series of spring-loaded, concentrically-arranged blades, situated between the front and rear elements of the lens, with which the whole shutter mechanism forms a unit. When the shutter is set to various speeds, i.e. 1/25th second, 1/50th second, and so on, springs are progressively tensioned and when the release button is pressed, the blades fly open from the centre, expand to the full diameter of the lens, then close rapidly. The shortest exposure with most such shutters is 1/500th second, though a few of the latest go up to 1/800th.

Coupled exposure meter

An exposure meter built into the camera body, or attached to it, and linked to the shutter speed dial. When the meter is activated, a pointer indicates the correct lens aperture for the shutter speed selected. Some such meters are 'crosscoupled', so that the lens diaphragm ring is turned direct. This obviates manual setting after reading the meter. Before use, the meter must be set to the ASA rating for the film in use.

Coupled film/ shutter wind

A useful facility for those who have to work fast, or are forgetful. A single stroke of a lever (a turn or two of a knob on some cameras) advances the film one frame, at the same time recocking the shutter.

Diaphragm

A series of concentric blades within the lens mount, which form a symmetrical opening at the centre. Turning a stop-ring or pointer to various stops alters the size of the aperture accordingly.

Double exposure prevention

A device which prevents more than one exposure being made on a single frame of film, and usually forming an integral part of the coupled film/shutter wind.

Elements

Modern lenses should rightly be called objectives, as a lens, properly speaking, is a single piece of glass. Thus, we may speak of a 5-glass construction, possibly compounded of two doublets and a single element. Usually, lenses of long focal length achieve good correction with less elements than those of shorter focal length. Very fast lenses (working at large apertures and thus passing a bright image, allowing exposure to be made in dim lighting conditions) require more elements to achieve the necessary corrections.

Exposure meter

A meter containing a light-sensitive cell of selenium or cadmium disulphide. It measures the light and translates this into terms of exposure. The CdS cell is more sensitive in dull light than the selenium cell, but only the more expensive CdS meters are as efficient as the best selenium meters.

Focal plane shutter

A curtain, or blind, with an adjustable slot, which makes the exposure by travelling across, and just in front of, the film. If such a shutter traverses the film in 1/100th second, and the slot is one-tenth the width of the frame, each part

of the film will receive 1/1000th second exposure. This is
an extremely accurate method of exposure, and is used in
nearly all modern miniature designs. When interchangeable lenses are·used, this system avoids the extra
expense and weight of having a separate shutter with
each lens.

Fully-automatic diaphragm (F.A.D.)

A facility which stops down the lens to the required
aperture for a brief instant just at the moment of exposure.
See *diaphragm,* and, for a fuller description of how F.A.D.
works, see *instant-return mirror.* S.A.D., semi-automatic
diaphragm, is all right for leisurely work, but F.A.D.
is almost essential in sports and press work. The term
applies only to single-lens reflex cameras.

Half-frame

A format on which the frames are vertical across the width
of the 35mm film, giving a frame-size approximately
2.5 × 1.7cm. In the hands of an expert this will produce
good results up to about 12.7 × 17.8cm prints, provided that
very distant subjects are avoided. However beautifully
made, such cameras should not be purchased by those
with leanings towards exhibition and competition work.

Helical focusing

The lens is moved backwards and forward by means of a
worm-screw in a tube construction. When the external
tube rotates with the action this may be a nuisance, as
lens hoods and filters rotate with it. On better-designed
instruments there is non-rotating helical focusing.

Instant-return mirror

On the eye-level single-lens reflex, pressing the
release button sets in motion a whole chain of actions.
First, the angled mirror flies up out of the light-path, and
blocks the light entering the camera through the eyepiece,
via the pentaprism. A striker-plate then comes forward
and pushes a pin protruding from the rear surface of the
lens-mount, thus stopping down the diaphragm. The
shutter then travels across the film, after which the
striker-plate releases its pressure, allowing the diaphragm
to open once more to full aperture, and the mirror drops
back to its 45° angle. Full, bright viewing of the subject in
the viewfinder is interrupted for a mere fraction of a
second. On older cameras, it was necessary to drop the

mirror manually after an exposure. When the mirror-return is automatic, as described, this is termed an instant-return mirror.

Interchangeable lenses

Many cameras have a single, fixed lens. The photographer is limited to the effects obtainable with this single focal length. This is not necessarily a disadvantage. Many fine and dramatic pictures are made on such instruments, and no time is wasted while the photographer (a) decides which lens to use, and (b) makes the change. Interchangeable lenses, however, do give the photographer the means of changing perspective, and thus the relationship between the various subjects in his composition, and the all-over relationship with the viewer. In addition, telephoto lenses enable the photographer to fill the frame with distant subjects and to take candid pictures from a distance. Wide-angle lenses enable him to include the whole scene in a restricted space.

Lines per millimetre

A phrase by which many a salesman dazzles the prospective purchaser of a lens. *This lens resolves 120 lines per m/m at the centre of the field,* for example. Stated thus baldly, the phrase is meaningless. It usually refers to the number of lines per m/m that can be visually resolved (with the aid of a magnifier) on a projected aerial image. Most film used in general photography is unable to record so many lines per m/m. Obviously, a film capable of recording 60 l.p.m. will produce the same degree of sharpness, whether the lens is capable of resolving 120 or only 60 l.p.m. In fact, optical scientists have now devised methods of describing lens performance which are more practical, but old advertising catch-phrases die hard. Most modern lenses of medium price are quite good enough for most purposes, and only produce markedly inferior results if the elements, through accidental damage or hasty assembly, are out of position.

Microprism

A group of tiny optical wedges at the centre of a focusing screen, used as an aid to sharp focusing. The wedges break up the image on the screen when the lens is not in focus. As the lens is brought into focus, the broken effect suddenly disappears.

Miniature

'Big' camera users regard all formats from 6×6 cm downwards as miniature. In practice miniature generally applies to cameras using 35mm film and having a frame size 36×24 mm. Such cameras are by no means always miniature in size. A jibe often levelled against the miniaturist is that he buys a small camera, but needs a suit-case to carry around all his accessories. In fact, if the user of a big camera were to equip himself with the same kind of accessories, he would require a truck to carry his suit-cases.

Pentaprism

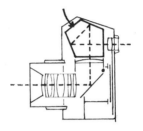

The five-sided prism around which the eye-level, single-lens reflex camera is constructed. The rays of light from the subject are focused by the lens, and reflected upwards via an angled mirror to the focusing screen. The pentaprism reflects the image at two further angles so that it may be observed horizontally through the viewfinder eyepiece. Thus, until the moment of exposure, the eye is able to see the same image that will fall on the film.

Pre-set stops

(Or pre-set diaphragm) A 'pre-set ring' is moved to the selected lens aperture, but does not actually alter the aperture, or 'stop'. In practice, the photographer is able to focus at full aperture at eye-level, then, without removing the camera from the eye, rotates the stop-ring until its movement is arrested by the pre-set ring.

Rangefinder

An optical device used to measure distance. In the *co-incident* type, two images appear, one overlapping the other. When these are made to coincide, the distance can be read off a scale. In the *split-image* type, a single image appears, divided into two halves, one of which is laterally offset. When the two halves are correctly aligned, the distance of the subject can be read off the scale. In a *coupled rangefinder* (C.R.F.) the moving control is linked to the camera lens, so that alignment of the image puts the lens automatically into correct focus. The rangefinder camera is to be preferred for press work in dim light, when using wide-angle lenses at large aperture. This is because SLR (single-lens reflex) focusing is less efficient with wide-angle lenses, particularly in dim light.

Self-resetting film counter

A counter which springs back to zero when the back of the camera is opened, and records the number of frames exposed as the film is advanced.

Semi-automatic diaphragm

(S.A.D.) After the diaphragm has been automatically stopped down by the same chain of actions that makes the exposure, it is necessary to reopen the diaphragm manually to the full diameter of the lens. See also *Fully-automatic diaphragm* and *Instant-return mirror.*

Single-lens reflex

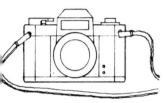

Also called SLR. In older-type instruments of this type, one looked down into a hood and observed the image reflected by a simple mirror on to a ground-glass screen. When the mirror was swung upwards, the same image was projected on to the film. In the modern SLR with pentaprism one views conveniently at eye-level. There are two great advantages to the SLR camera. One is freedom from parallax, which is viewing error caused by the different viewpoints of a lens and viewfinder on other types of camera. At very close distances, parallax error becomes acute. The other advantage is that the effects of different focal length lenses at various apertures can be seen at once.

6cm X 6cm (2¼″ square)

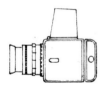

An extremely popular size among advanced amateurs and professionals concerned with higher technical quality than *they* can obtain with 35mm materials. Notice that I do not say that *can* be obtained, for it is a fact that some people are able to produce the highest quality work on 35mm film, whereas others, producing superb work on larger sizes, will never feel at home with 35mm. 6 × 6cm reaches peak perfection in such cameras as the Rolleiflex and Mamiyaflex (see *Twin-lens reflex*), and the Hasselblad and Practisix (see *Single-lens reflex*). The square format means that the camera can be held always in the upright position, but there is good space on the frame to compose horizontally or vertically, as well as square.

Stops, or f numbers

The numbers represent the percentage of light transmission (of the whole lens) when the diaphragm aperture is set at different sizes. These numbers are often confusing to the novice, as the largest number

for around £500 you get the highest quality in 35mm rangefinder cameras:
the Leica M5 with 50mm Summicron *f*2 lens

Konica C35 is a 'new generation' camera. Built-in electric eye operates linked shutter speeds and lens apertures on a sliding scale from 1/600th at *f*16 down to 1/30th at *f*2.8. Just focus by rangefinder and press the button. All for around £52

(say, f22) represents the smallest aperture. Conversely, the smallest number (say, f1·4) represents the largest aperture. The usual stop numbers found on modern lenses are:

f1·4   f2   f2·8   f4   f5·6   f8   f11   f16   f22

Each larger aperture lets through twice as much light as the next smaller. Thus, f4 gives twice as bright an image as f5·6; f5·6 gives eight times as bright an image as 16, and so on. f1·4 is considered very fast, but a well-corrected lens of this aperture costs a great deal of money. f2 or 1·8 is adequate, and less costly, for most subjects – even fast action photography in dim light. f2·8 should not be considered slow, however, and is, indeed, often the largest aperture on lenses used to cover formats larger than 35mm.

Sub-miniature

A very small negative size, often on 16mm film. It has its amateur advocates, largely on account of novelty value, but cannot compete with larger film sizes for serious work.

Through-the-lens (TTL) meter

Light-sensitive cells, usually aligned one on either side of the focusing screen of the SLR measure the brightness of the image passed by the lens. Turning the stop-ring or the shutter speed dial will centre a pointer visible in the viewfinder window, thus setting the correct exposure. A minor disadvantage of this system is that the whole camera must be handled every time an exposure reading is made. This is avoided when a separate meter is used, but the TTL system is undoubtedly a time-saver.

Twin-lens reflex

The original design was embodied in the Rolleiflex. It is basically two cameras, one above the other, each with one of a matched pair of lenses. The upper camera body contains a mirror fixed at an angle of 45°, which reflects the image up to a ground-glass screen inside a hood. Bringing this into focus automatically focuses the lower lens, which passes the image direct to the film. At close distances, there is a disadvantage of parallax error (see *Single-lens reflex)* but provision is usually made to offset this.

2. Focusing

Focal length

If you hold a magnifying lens over a sheet of paper and raise it slowly, there comes a point at which the sun's rays are brought together at a single point. The distance between the glass and the paper at this point is the focal length of the lens.

Camera lenses work the same way. It is generally accepted that the correct, or standard, focal length (i.e. one that will render the subject with 'normal' or 'pleasing' perspective) for a given film size, approximates the diagonal of the format. Thus, the standard focal length for the 35mm camera (format approximately 36mm × 24mm) is 50-55mm. The standard focal length for the 6 × 6cm format on 120-size film is 75-80mm.

The infinity mark

Imagine that we are focusing the camera, by means of screen or rangefinder, on a distant church spire. At the distance from the film at which the spire appears to be sharply defined, the lens is said to be set at *Infinity*. This film-lens distance corresponds to the focal length of the lens. The infinity mark, which represents the ultimate setting on the distance scale, is shown as Inf., or by the symbol ∞ .

On small cameras the infinity mark is set at about 15-23m and any subject beyond this distance will be sharp enough on the film for general photographic purposes.

As the camera and the subject move closer together, it becomes necessary to alter the focus. The lens has to be moved progressively farther from the film in order to maintain sharp focus on the subject.

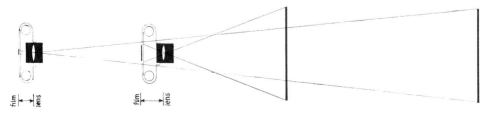

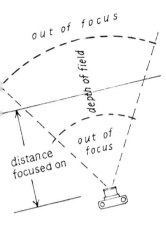

(1) With any given lens, set at any given distance, theoretically true focus is achieved only at the exact point focused on. In practice, though, there will be an area of adequate sharpness on either side of the plane of true focus. This area, reaching both towards and away from the camera, is called the *depth of field*.
(2) Other things being equal (i.e. lens aperture and distance setting) a lens of long focal length has less depth of field than a lens of shorter focal length.
(3) The depth of field increases as the lens aperture is reduced.
(4) At any given aperture, the depth of field increases with the distance of the subject.
(5) Depth of field is greater beyond the subject than towards the camera.

this page and 21 and 23 (top): prints from colour shots by Peter Goodliffe demonstrate the meaning of depth of field

here the figure is only a small, but important, part of the scene, all of which is in focus at f11 (35mm lens)

the photographer changes to a 50mm lens. The model comes in closer. But at f11 she is still mixed up with the architecture . . .

. . . open up to f2 (increasing the shutter speed) and we have a girl with an elegant but unobtrusive background. It still isn't quite right . . .

These five related points suggest a few rules for general photography:

(a) If we wish to obtain sharp focus both near to, and far from, the camera, a small lens aperture should be chosen, preferably in conjunction with a lens of short focal length.

(b) If the background to our subject is bitty and confusing, the use of a wide lens aperture, preferably in conjunction with a lens of longer-than-average focal length, will throw the background out of focus and give sharp relief to the subject itself.

(c) Where focusing is difficult or impossible, as in the case of a rapidly approaching car, it is useful to focus beforehand (pre-focus) on a given point, and press the shutter release as the subject reaches that point.

The ground-glass screen

Screen focusing calls for judgment on the part of the photographer. Using a ground-glass screen, as employed in single- and twin-lens reflex cameras, one racks the lens back and forth, observing the subject coming into, and going out of, focus. These 'arcs' of focusing get shorter and shorter until a point is reached at which one is unable to define a sharper degree of focus. To reduce human error to a minimum, a magnifying lens, or a microprism, or both, are incorporated into the viewing system. The ground-glass screen, nevertheless, provides a negative method of focusing.

Screen focusing is easiest with lenses of normal or moderately long focal length. In dim light focusing becomes more difficult, particularly with lenses of extreme focal length. In such cases one is often reduced to the expedient of estimating the distance and setting it by scale.

The coupled rangefinder

twin image

split image

When using a coupled rangefinder, on the other hand, no human judgment is required. Twin- or split-images are brought together, and at this point the lens has been brought to precise focus. Focusing, in other words, is positive. Thus, for press and 'available light' work, especially where wide-angle lenses are constantly in use at large apertures in dim light, the rangefinder camera has important advantages.

From this, it might appear that rangefinder focusing is always to be preferred to screen focusing, but this would

a successful portrait resulted from the use of a long-focus lens with wide aperture, which made sure of a shallow depth of field

pre-focus, then wait for the right moment (HP4 film)

be wrong. From the compositional point of view, screen focusing is unsurpassed. It allows the photographer to see just what he is getting on his film. With a single-lens reflex camera, the photographer can also study the effect of depth of field at various apertures, and the perspective changes afforded by lenses of differing focal lengths.

In the rangefinder design, where one is looking through a viewfinder, this is not possible, and one relies more on knowledge and experience.

Aperture

Every lens has a maximum aperture, and these apertures are also called, by English-speaking photographers, stops or f numbers. On modern small cameras the maximum lens aperture may be $f2·8$, $f2$, or even $f1·4$, which is a very large aperture indeed. Some lenses will be marked $f1·8$ or $f1·9$ instead of $f2$, and for practical purposes such slight differences can be ignored.

Each larger aperture lets through twice as much light as the next smaller in an arithmetical progression. A similar arithmetical progression applies to the range of shutter speeds, i.e. 1/30th second, 1/60th second, 1/125th second, and so on. Where the arithmetical series of lens apertures is considered in conjunction with the shutter speeds, we speak of a reciprocal relationship. This will be dealt with in the next chapter. For the moment, let us deal with the effect of lens apertures on focusing.

We cannot place a person 1.5m in front of the camera, 457m in front of a view, and hope to get both subjects sharply focused together. We have seen, however, that stopping the lens well down (i.e. reducing the aperture through which the image passes) can bring us very close to getting both near and far objects into sharp focus.

This would suggest to many people that differential focusing is a waste of time. Why not simply set the lens for the middle distance, stop down to the smallest aperture, and obtain sharp focus near and far?

A good idea as far as it goes, but—it must be remembered that the more one reduces the aperture of the lens, the less light will be passed to the film. By way of compensation, the speed of the shutter must be reduced, too.

If we were photographing a horse jumping, we should need a shutter speed of about 1/500th second to stop the action. Unless the sun were shining brightly, a fairly large lens aperture would be called for.

Again, if we try to use a very small lens aperture in dull lighting conditions, our shutter speed may have to be reduced to 1/30th second or even slower, with greater attendant risk of moving the camera slightly during exposure, and blurring the image.

A fast shutter speed, therefore, helps to make sharp pictures, just as much as careful focusing, but it also entails the use of large apertures in dull weather.

Zone focusing

The 'ever-ready' camera, so called, is never ready for action until properly focused and the exposure set. When the light is good, the man who keeps a sharp lookout for a sudden picture may set his lens for an average distance, say, 4.6m, and stop the lens down to an aperture that will give reasonable sharpness over a considerable area.

Many a brilliant 'slice of life' has been shot this way, while the careful technician was still making measurements. The figures below suggest three such zone focusing distances for a 50 mm lens which will cover a great many situations.

focus 2m at *f*8

zone A

field 1.8m to 2.7m

focus 3.7m at *f*11

zone B

field 2.7m to 4.9m

focus ∞ at *f*16

zone C

field 3.7m to infinity

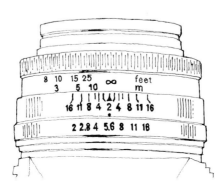

distance →

depth of field →

f numbers →

3. Exposing

Exposure, in the photographic context, is the length of time during which we allow the light to reach the film. Inside most film cartons a simple exposure guide is given for the film in use. Thus, on the leaflet accompanying say, an Agfa CT18 colour film, we find the following useful little chart:

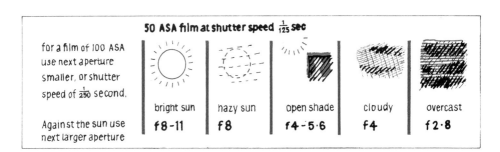

for a film of 100 ASA use next aperture smaller, or shutter speed of $\frac{1}{250}$ second.	**50 ASA film at shutter speed $\frac{1}{125}$ sec**				
	bright sun	hazy sun	open shade	cloudy	overcast
Against the sun use next larger aperture	f8-11	f8	f4-5·6	f4	f2·8

In the lighting conditions shown, provided one uses a shutter speed of 1/125th second, brilliant colour transparencies will result. For summer holidays and casual photography many people never feel the need for anything more complicated than this.

It will be realized that such a table depends for its simplicity on the fact that all variables have been eliminated. A single shutter speed is used, and this relates only to the sensitivity of Agfa CT18 film, which is 50 ASA.

Exposure tables and calculators

Exposure tables and calculators, usually in the form of plastic dials, are an extension of the above simple table. On a calculator, one pre-sets the ASA rating for the film in use, lines this up against a description of the subject and lighting conditions, and then reads off the correct aperture for any selected shutter speed.

Although more versatile than the leaflet enclosed with the film, a calculator is not more accurate. For the beginner, the leaflet may even be preferable, as the possibility of wrong choice is eliminated.

Exposure meters

Exposure meters actually measure the brightness of the light, and thus relieve the user from guessing which printed description (on a table or calculator) best matches the scene before him.

Exposure meters are actuated by either a selenium cell or a cadmium disulphide cell (CdS cell). The former reacts directly to light and the better-quality instruments will function perfectly for a lifetime. The CdS meter is activated by a tiny battery, which needs replacing periodically (about once a year in normal use).

CdS meters are more highly sensitive than selenium meters, and are thus more useful for 'available light' photography indoors. Only the best of them, however, have the same all-over response as the selenium meter, which closely follows that of the human eye.

There are three types of exposure meter in general use, reflected light meters, incident light meters, and those which are adaptable to both systems of measurement.

Reflected light readings

The meter cell is pointed at the subject and measures the amount of light reflected from it. This is both quick and accurate provided there are not violent differences in tone between the various parts of the subject.

When photographing a landscape, point the meter slightly downwards, so that not more than one-third of the sky is included in the meter's field of view. If too much of the bright sky were included the meter would give an inflated reading and we would under-expose the important tones in the foreground.

Where a subject does contain strong contrasts we must add some common-sense interpretation to the blind reaction of the meter.

Let us take a sunlit colonnade. One side of each column gleams white, the other is in intense shadow. Close-up readings may show that the shadow side requires fifty times as much exposure as the sunlit side. For example, 1/250th second on the bright side, 1/5th second on the shadow side. The best compromise in this case would be to give an exposure midway between the two extremes, i.e. about 1/30th second.

The highlit area will be over-exposed and the shadow area under-exposed and thus, in the finished print, there will be detail in neither. But, we will successfully have retained the glaring contrast of the colonnade. This is a practical compromise.

Until recently, academic teaching would have abhorred such advice. It was necessary to retain 'a full range of tones' in every subject. Modern photography, however, is a servant, not a master, to the effects we wish to translate on to paper or transparency.

When photographing a girl wearing a black dress in bright sunlight, we would use our reflected light meter differently. A compromise reading here would be nonsensical. The dress would remain as black as ever, and the bright, white face would be featureless. Consequently, we would go in close, take a reading of the face tones from a few centimetres away (being careful not to cast the shadow of hand or meter on to the face) and stick to the reading obtained.

Thus, general rules for the successful use of reflected light meters are:

1. Provided light and dark areas are fairly evenly balanced, a direct reading of the whole scene will do.

2. If it is necessary to retain some shadow detail as well as some highlight detail, take two readings — one of the darkest shadow area in which it is important to retain detail; another of the brightest highlight in which it is important to retain detail. Choose an exposure setting midway between the two. Through inexperience you may choose highlight and shadow readings covering a greater brightness range than the film can cope with. In practice, the film will solve the problem for you by doing what it can. Later, a choice of a soft grade of printing paper will compress contrast and give a pleasing print.

3. Where a face is prominent in the picture space, expose for this only. This is particularly important when colour film is in use, as flesh tones must not be falsified.

Substitute reading

Assume for a moment that you are standing three metres from a person, but by means of a telephoto lens intend to make a head-and-shoulder portrait. The face *is brightly lit by the sun,* but the background is in shadow. Your exposure meter used from 3m away sees a large dark area with a small bright face at its centre. The reading, therefore, would be almost correct for the dark background, but would render the face very over-exposed.

A fence prevents you getting any closer to your subject, so how do you obtain a correct reading for the face? Simply, by what is known as a substitute measurement, or reading.

Hold up your hand, so that the light is falling on it from the same angle as on the face. Bring the meter within a few centimetres of your hand and take a reading from it. Be careful not to cast a shadow from the meter itself. This reading will be correct for the portrait three metres away.

When you are photographing in sunlight, your distance from the light source is the same as that of the subject, so the substitute reading will be correct, but with artificial light sources one must be more careful. If the main light source, for example, were reaching your hand from a distance of 3.7m, the reading would be much higher than at a subject position 5.5m away.

Incident light readings

Here, the cell of the meter is covered with a white plastic hemisphere, or cone. Instead of pointing the meter at the subject, it is pointed from the subject position towards the camera position. Used this way, it measures the light falling on the subject, not reflected from it.

Metrastar: typical of a new generation of CdS meters for both reflected and incident light measurements

Such a reading of incident light, it will readily be seen, will not fluctuate according to the bright or dark tones of the subject matter.

Incident light readings are so balanced that they always give correct exposure for skin tones. They are thus of great value to the colour portraitist. Used for general photography they are particularly useful for exposure determination in cases of extreme contrast, as they provide an average without the necessity for making separate readings of highlight and shadow detail.

There are one or two situations in which an incident light reading cannot be made.

Suppose you are in the dark interior of a church, and wish to photograph the transilluminated stained glass windows. Only a reflected light reading can do this, and incident light meters are provided with a reflected light attachment (to replace the hemisphere or cone) for such a situation.

The distant view with haze is another case in point. There will be a greater concentration of haze between subject and camera, than between the incident light meter and camera. This haze is usually a light 'magnifier', and such readings tend to cause over-exposure.

A good rule for the owners of incident light meters is to use incident light for near- and middle-distance pictures, reflected light for distant views.

Nowadays, most of the better quality instruments, whether designed basically for reflected or incident light measurement, have a means of conversion. Either the white plastic hemisphere is slid across, or away from, the meter's cell, or a separate attachment is provided.

On all meters it is first necessary to set a scale for the ASA rating (measure of sensitivity) of the film in use. Once this setting has been made, however, it need not be altered until a film of higher or lower sensitivity is used.

the Weston Master – the most
popular light meter

Photographs provided by Kodak laboratories
show: top left, overexposure (a flat, lifeless
result); top right, underexposed (dense shadows
and excessive contrast. Right, correct exposure
gives lively 'colour' and good balance of
light and dark

4. Choice of films

Choice of black and white films

To start off with, let us get the use of black and white and colour films into a proper perspective. Colour film has *not* superseded black and white film, and neither is the use of colour film always to be preferred.

Some pictures derive their effectiveness from the interrelationship of lines and shapes, of light and shade. The addition of colour may be not only superfluous, but may actually detract from the effectiveness. In other words, the black and white picture, used properly, forms an abstraction of what was essentially pictorial in the subject, and avoids the purely coincidental distraction of colour.

At the other extreme, a picture may contain no bold forms or contrasts, and depend for its effectiveness entirely on subtle, pastel hues. Reduced to shades of grey, such a picture would be meaningless.

Between the two extremes is a mighty range of subjects and situations which lend themselves to treatment in either black and white or colour.

It is simplest to classify these under four headings:
(1) Slow films (ASA 25–50)
(2) Medium speed films (ASA 80–125)
(3) Fast films (ASA 400)
(4) Super speed films (ASA 800–1250)

Slow films

These have the finest grain and are thus capable of the greatest degree of enlargement without any break-up of image quality.

Because of its relatively low sensitivity, such film calls for moderate shutter speeds and often wide lens apertures, even in bright light. Pictorially, this can be an advantage. Use of a wide aperture limits the depth of field to the subject itself. A distracting background is thrown completely out of focus, and the subject stands out boldly against it. This is called differential focusing, and is not possible when using fast film in bright light, as small lens apertures (and great depth of field) are then unavoidable.

35mm Agfa IFF was used for this static close-up with studio lighting

The slow films provided by most makers are quite contrasty, and sometimes call for special development if harshness is to be avoided. The exceptions are in the Agfa range. Agfa IFF (25 ASA) and Agfa IF (40 ASA) have a softer gradation than their counterparts from other makers.

The serious worker, intent on superb technical quality outdoors, will often find himself needing a firm tripod, as even moderate stopping down of the lens may call for exposures too slow to be safely hand-held.

For the highest technical quality, as in copying and scientific photography, slow film should always be used. It is the best choice for still-life subjects, where the use of a tripod and long exposure is no problem.

Medium speed films

These are best for 95 per cent of the requirements of most amateur photographers. Properly exposed and carefully processed, they will yield prints of exhibition quality even from 35mm negatives. Professionals, other than press photographers, invariably choose films of medium speed for everything apart from action photography in dim light.

Although less fine grained than slower films, the degree of visible granularity in the final *print* will depend on a number of incidental factors. many of which are under the photographer's control. In certain conditions (see page 81), a 40.6 × 50.8cm enlargement from a film of medium speed may appear to be of the same technical quality as a similar enlargement made from a more fine-grained film.

Generally, the inherent contrast of films decreases as their speed increases (this, of course, refers to ASA speed, or sensitivity, not shutter speed). Thus, most medium speed films are less contrasty than slow films. This provides more tolerance under contrasty lighting conditions.

At the same time, medium speed film is not too fast to allow differential focusing. Provided a fast shutter speed is used, one may manage large apertures (with limited depth of field) even in bright light.

a French landscape on FP4, 35mm

delicious textures, adequately recorded on the medium speed Ilford FP4

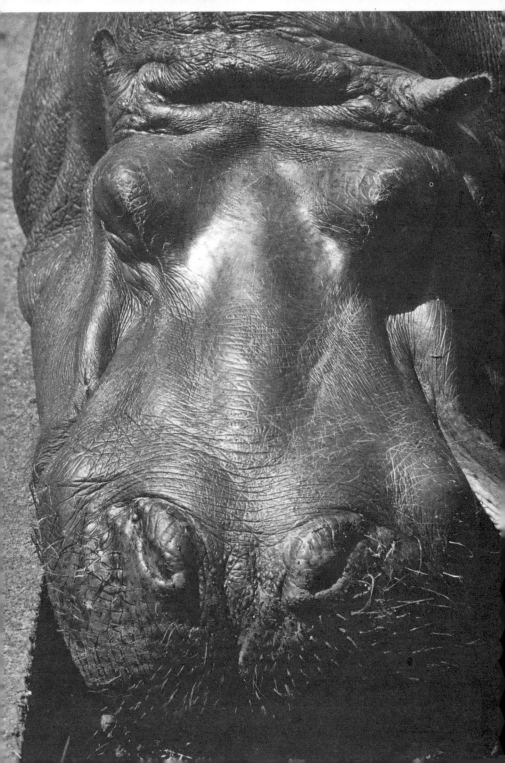

Fast films

These are represented by such emulsions as Kodak Tri-X, Ilford HP4, and Agfapan 400. Nominally rated at 400 ASA, they are the standard material used by press photographers, photo-journalists, and all those wishing to capture living subjects by whatever light happens to be present (available light).

This versatility is achieved by the film manufacturer at the expense of two other qualities — fineness of grain, and the ability to reproduce very fine detail. It must be pointed out, however, that the essence of such photography — action, emotion, expression, mood and situation — seldom depends on the reproduction of fine detail.

Although definitely more grainy than medium speed or slow films, these modern fast films are nevertheless of quite reasonable grain. Even in 35mm size, if the enlargement is to be no more than 20.3 × 25.4cm, the difference should not show.

Made from a good negative, even a 30.5 × 38.1cm enlargement would not betray the use of fast film if a lustre-surfaced paper were used (this 'swallows' much of the grain that would be revealed on a glossy-surfaced print). Thus much of the argument against the use of fast film becomes purely academic.

opposite: Agfa ISS

always keep an eye open for that combination of colour and character that produces really satisfying holiday pictures. Most audiences at home slide shows prefer these to general views. Agfa CT18. Taken with a 105mm lens on a Pentax

In the past, all fast films conformed to the general 'rule', the faster the film the softer the gradation. This is no longer true. One film in particular, Kodak Tri-X, is just as contrasty as the average film of medium speed.

High Speed Ektachrome Type B is balanced for artificial light and has a nominal ASA rating of 125. Here it has been used at 500 ASA, allowing an exposure of 1/250 second at f2.8. Used this way, first development has to be increased, and some independent processors will undertake this kind of 'push' processing

Super speed films

These are special emulsions intended solely for press photography at very low light levels, i.e. floodlit football, jazz cellars, and so on.

Undoubtedly, the grain is very coarse, but only by comparison with slower film stock. Allowing speeds of 1000 ASA (Agfapan 1000) and even faster, 1600 ASA upwards (Kodak 2475), such films should be chosen for special purposes only.

They are frequently resorted to by graphic artists and advertising photographers to achieve the outstanding grainy images required for certain effects.

To sum up:

Slow films for technical or leisurely work.
Medium films for general photography.
Fast films for 'life' photography.
Super speed films for action at very low light levels.

In general

It is useful to have a 'repertoire' of films to cover a great variety of situations, but the photographer who keeps chopping and changing films is inviting the disaster of unfamiliarity.

The professional soon learns to work 95 per cent of the time with a single type of film. He becomes thoroughly familiar with this film, knows how it will behave in all circumstances, and how to control it in processing. He is thus able to produce consistent and reliable work. He changes film stock only for a very special purpose.

Few photographers ever need consider more than two types of black and white film. One's first choice should depend on the kind of work one is mainly concerned with. If this is action photography, the number one film will be a fast one, with occasional use of a slow film for the odd technical job that crops up.

For the outdoor photographer of general subjects, a medium speed film will be number one choice. This will cope with still-life and all but the most exacting technical job. Very occasionally, a slower or faster film may be needed for a special job.

opposite: the newspaper photographer might use flash to make sure, but this 1250 ASA picture has more realism than flash could give

Strong reds tend to be flattened and to 'jump forward' in colour films – but this is all right when the whole subject is red. The quality of this 6cm-square transparency is at its best in projection

Colour films

There are two main types: reversal and negative. Reversal provides a transparency, for direct viewing or projection. Negative provides a colour negative from which colour prints or enlargements can be made direct.

Colour prints can be made from transparencies, but this calls for the manufacture of an intermediate negative (interneg) and adds to the expense.

Colour transparencies may also be made from colour negatives, but are never as good as original colour transparencies.

Because light shines through it, a transparency can reproduce a vastly greater range of brightnesses than a print on paper. An average brightness range for a transparency may be 5000 : 1, whereas on a paper print it can hardly exceed 30 : 1. This is why the amateur so often speaks of transparencies as 'breathtaking', but finds colour prints disappointing.

In fact, the production of a good colour print calls for a very specialized appreciation of the use of colour over a limited brightness range.

After exposure, a reversal colour film is developed and reversed. The finished transparency is, in fact, a negative which has undergone reversal. The exposure in the camera, therefore, must be very accurate.

The negative colour film, on the other hand, is only the first step in a two-part process. The negative is first obtained, and a certain degree of control and correction is possible at the printing stage. Thus, a bluish cast that might spoil a transparency can be eliminated during the negative—positive process.

Colour temperature

An understanding of colour temperature is basic to a proper understanding and use of colour materials. The phrase sounds a little forbidding, but it is merely a label for a quite simple concept.

We all know what we mean by temperature, as related to atmosphere or radiant heat. Rising temperature, rising heat; falling temperature, lessening heat.

Also, we all know what is meant by 'warm' light, and 'cold' light, though the adjectives now are used to describe colour. We could speak of blue as a cold colour, orange and red as warm and even hot colours.

This is the meaning of colour temperature. To describe colour temperature more accurately, we use the Kelvin Scale, and speak of light of a certain quality as 'so many degrees Kelvin'.

A few of the photographically more important light sources are given below, together with their position on the Kelvin Scale.

Clear blue sky	10,000° K.
Midday sun and sky } Electronic flash }	6,000° K.
Noon sunlight	5,600° K.
Photoflood lamp	3,400° K.
Studio lamp	3,200° K.
100-watt lamp	2,860° K.

You will notice that a high Kelvin number relates to a colder colour temperature, and, conversely, that a low Kelvin number relates to a warmer colour temperature.

The Kelvin Scale is based on what is known scientifically as a black body radiator. Imagine that we are about to put a cold, black poker into a hot fire. At first, the cold poker radiates no heat and is colourless. As it heats up, it first glows dark red, then bright red, then orange, yellow, white, and finally blue.

As the heat increases the colour becomes colder and this is what the Kelvin Scale enables us to describe.

The surprise of colour

The human eye is a sensory extension of the human brain, and therefore has a sizeable 'think' mechanism behind it. When the eye sees a girl whose face has a greenish cast because the skin is reflecting the grass on which she is lying, the mind often fails to notice the phenomenon. The mind well knows that normal flesh tones appear to be a healthy, creamy colour, and, unless it is trained to see *actually* rather than *intellectually*, 'refuses' the green cast on the face.

The colour film, on the other hand, accepts what the lens gives it without argument. Hence, we are often taken by surprise when the colour film reveals the true state of affairs.

In fact, no object has any colour until light falls on it, and the quality of the colour depends entirely on the kind of light.

Being the accommodating process that it is, the see/think mechanism is able to accept whatever it sees, whatever the the colour temperature of the light falling on it. But the unthinking colour film has to be 'balanced' in manufacture to produce an end result that approximates to what the average human can accept as 'normal'.

For this reason, every manufacturer supplies each of his transparency films in two types; one is balanced for use in daylight, the other for use by tungsten or photoflood lighting.

Compensating filters

A large range of colour compensating filters is made, designed to moderate the colour temperature of the scene before us to that for which the film in use is balanced.

By way of example. We have in the camera a daylight-type colour film balanced for average noon sunlight (about 5,600° K.). We are photographing a landscape illuminated by sunlight from a clear blue sky without clouds. The colour temperature of such light is colder (possibly 10,000° K.) than that for which the film was balanced. To effect the shift from 10,000° K. down to 5,600° K., we would slip a warm-coloured filter over the lens. This could be a Wratten 81a (pale brown) filter, or equivalent by another maker.

Only the commercial photographer coping with a vast amount of varied colour work will ever need as many as half a dozen compensating filters. The average photographer can get by quite happily with only two: a UV (ultra violet absorbing filter) which appears colourless but counteracts a slight blue cast when an excess of UV light is present, and an 81a (pale brown) which will pleasantly warm up even the coldest scene. The UV filter requires no exposure increase, the 81a needs an extra third of a stop exposure.

Even under the bluest sky, the practical worker will seldom find he needs a browner filter than the 81a, though several are made.

Some colour film manufacturers recommend that a pale blue filter (82a) be used within two hours of sunrise or sunset, as the light is then yellower than at noon. While technically true, this is a matter of taste. By filtering the yellowish light one destroys the very effect of warmth that attracted one to making the picture.

A colour correction filter enables one to use daylight-type film by artificial light, and vice versa. An 80a filter is used to correct daylight-type colour film for tungsten light (3,100° K.– 3,200° K.) and an 80b filter for photoflood lights (3,300° K.– 3,400° K.). These filters are dark blue. However, the use of daylight-type film in artificial light with a blue filter should be reserved for emergencies only. An unpleasant greenish cast is usually present. Artificial light film used in daylight with the appropriate filter gives far more pleasant results and for such a film, intended for tungsten light, an 85b filter is required. Certain films (Kodachrome II) are balanced for photoflood lighting, and an 85 filter will correct these for daylight use. These filters are dark brown.

One good compromise, which avoids the necessity for carrying two kinds of film, is to load with Agfa CK20 colour film. By tungsten light this colour film has the useful speed of 80 ASA, with considerably more sharpness than other fast colour films. Used by daylight with an 85 filter it is free from blue cast and has a speed of 40 ASA.

Daylight colour films	sun	blue skylight or cold daylight	very bluish shadows	very warm daylight – near sunrise or sunset	electronic and blue flashbulbs	clear flashbulbs
Kodachrome II Kodachrome X	none	1a (skylight)	81A (cloudy)	82A (morning and evening)	none	not recommended
Ektachrome HS Ektachrome X	none	ditto	ditto	ditto	none	80D (flash)

Artificial light colour films	photoflood No. 1	studio lamps	room lighting	daylight, electronic and blue flashbulbs	clear flashbulbs
Kodachrome IIA	none	82A	82A	85	81C
Ektachrome HS Type B	81A (cloudy) none	none	none satisfactory	85B	81C

Which shall I choose?

Colour films by different makers have different characteristics, but what is, or is not, pleasing colour rendering, is finally a matter of opinion.

I mentioned pleasing colour, not accurate colour. Only in scientific photographs may it be essential to reproduce faithfully the colours of an original. Even the copying of paintings for reproduction seldom achieves visual accuracy. In general work, the rule is to find a film that suits you, and stick to it.

As with black and white film, faster colour films are grainier than slower ones. For technical work the slower films (about 25 ASA) should be chosen, and these are often preferred by holidaymakers whose photography is confined, for the most part, to sunshine.

The films of 50–64 ASA are more generally useful, with very little increase in granularity. On the average projection screen, for example, it is hardly possible to tell the difference between slow and medium speed colour films by the granular appearance alone.

High speed colour films (normally between 125 ASA and 200 ASA) should be reserved for action photography. Although the colour is often soft and pleasing, grain can be disturbing and transparencies will not be as sharp as those obtained with slower materials.

indoor snapshots are possible on the relatively low-speed colour films. This early-morning tricycle-rider was lit by a narrow shaft of sunlight. Kodachrome II, f2 1/60 second

5. Lenses and accessories

Many prize-winning photographs are taken with a fixed-lens camera, which confines the photographer to the use of a single focal length. In fact, quite a number of professional photographers never feel the need for interchangeable lenses. This points up the fact, which will be dealt with in Chapter 11, that the photographer with a 'seeing eye' can make good pictures with anything – even an old box camera.

Conversely, the possession of half a dozen lenses will not make for good pictures if the eye behind the viewfinder sees unimaginatively.

Further lenses may be added to one's outfit, for special purposes, but there is no need to assume that a subject ideally suited to, say, a 135mm lens, cannot be successfully taken with a 105mm lens, and vice versa.

A good rule is not to equip oneself with more than the minimum number of lenses necessary for the kind of work undertaken.

Making the right choice

Having started an outfit with a lens of standard focal length (50–55mm) the miniature camera user wonders what his second choice should be. Ought he to buy a 105mm or a 135mm lens? Or would a wide-angle lens be more useful a choice?

For the photographer whose main interest will be portraiture, an obvious second choice would be a lens of 85–105mm focal length. This will give pleasing perspective when filling the frame with a head-and-shoulders.

If one's portraiture is to be of the candid, available light variety, a wide aperture lens ($f1\cdot9$–$f2\cdot8$) of this focal length would be ideal. In the 6 × 6cm format, an equivalent lens would be about 180mm focal length.

If one's main interest is in landscape and pictorial photography, one of the 35mm focal length lenses is suggested as first choice. This allows the background to be balanced by an object large in the foreground (the village street balanced by a close-up of the village pump) and with sufficient depth of field to get both sharply in focus.

Choice chart   Reference to the Choice chart will assist in selecting the most generally useful focal lengths for different kinds of photography.

Filling the frame   An argument often advanced by big camera enthusiasts is that their negatives have to be enlarged less than smaller sizes, and will therefore produce better quality prints. A good big 'un, the argument goes, is better than a good little 'un.

Because of this, the quality-conscious miniaturist learns to fill the frame, as far as possible, with the essential part of his subject. This avoids the necessity for enlarging small parts of the negative.

Longer focal length lenses, especially when used for the photography of distant subjects, enable one to achieve this result. According to its degree of magnification, the long focal length lens brings the distant object close.

Lens quality   The ideal lens gives a well-contrasted image, with fine definition from edge to edge of the negative, even at wide apertures.

It is easier to obtain good contrast in a lens of moderate focal length than in one of very long focal length (at a distance, aerial haze intervenes to cut contrast). On the other hand, it is optically easier to achieve edge-to-edge sharpness on a long focal length lens.

Only fairly expensive lenses come close to achieving the best of both worlds. A vast number of cheap lenses are on the market, mostly manufactured in Japan. These are built down to a price, rather than up to a specification, and the intending purchaser is well advised to try out such a lens before purchasing. On the face of it, a lens of very large aperture may appear to be a better buy than a similarly-priced one of the same focal length but more modest aperture. This is seldom so. At the same price, the manufacturer has probably been able to build more quality into the lens of modest aperture.

The more expensive Japanese lenses, of course, are world renowned for high performance.

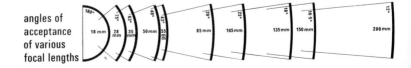

angles of
acceptance
of various
focal lengths

copies of colour transparencies by Peter Goodliffe show the acute difference between the angles of view of a 500 and a 28mm lens – taken from exactly the same position

a long lens is almost a must at air displays and fetes. This was taken with a 200mm lens at 1/1000 second, using Fujichrome R100 film

Lenses in practice

The worker who wants to be ready to take pictures at all times, and with a minimum of fuss, will consider other things as well as focal length. What, for instance, is the diameter of his lenses? If he has an outfit consisting of 35mm, 50mm, and 90mm lenses, it saves much time, and duplication of equipment, if one filter will fit all three lenses.

He may be tempted to pay an extra couple of pounds for an attractive leather case with sling, designed for each of his lenses. Such cases are a waste of time, and a less practical way of carrying lenses could not have been devised!

Far better to have the lenses ready for instant use in separate compartments of a gadget bag.

Filters

There are two kinds. Ordinary colour filters, used to alter the tones in black and white photography, and colour compensating filters, used to adjust the colour temperature of the light to that for which the colour film was balanced (see Chapter 4, *Choice of films*).

Colour filters for black and white photography: the most useful is undoubtedly the 2X yellow. This gives good rendering of skies and generally brightens a landscape or view.

Darker yellow filters, with a factor of 4X, add to the contrast of a scene and render skies dramatically.

Orange filters, with a factor of about 5X, give an even more

right filter, wrong moment: an orange filter has produced a bright cloud at the masthead and a black gasworks on the shore. But the sky does look blue . . . Kodak Plus X film

pronounced effect. Brickwork stands out brightly against very dark skies. This filter should be avoided if faces are prominent in the picture, as skin tones tend towards an unhealthy whiteness. This is also true, to a lesser extent, with yellow filters.

Red filters, up to a factor of 10X or more, blacken blue skies, and give dramatic contrast. Once very popular among salon photographers for landscape work, this effect is now considered somewhat dated. Red filters are used by commercial photographers to bring out the grain pattern in furniture.

Outdoor photographers who often combine figures with landscape, often prefer a green filter, factor about 3X, to a yellow. The darkening effect on skies is similar to that obtained with the yellow filter, but skin tones are darker and healthier. In every case the exposure must be increased (see chart page 26).

A word of warning. Many beginners are tempted to collect several of these attractive circles of coloured glass. Far better to buy just the two suggested, and add to the collection only when the occasion arises — if ever.

a sequence of portraits – same girl, same bridge – demonstrate the control over composition and the different perspectives given by interchangeable lenses. Copies from colour shots by Peter Goodliffe

at 0.9m, lens: 28mm

at 1.5m, lens: 50mm

at 3m, lens: 105mm

at 15m, lens: 500mm

A minimum outfit

A minimum outfit that will cope with most general photography consists of a camera with a single lens, a lens hood, a 2X (two times) yellow filter, a UV or Skylight filter, and an exposure meter.

The lens hood protects the lens from light-rays outside its field of view, avoiding 'flare', and helping to maintain good image contrast.

The yellow filter used with black and white film darkens blue skies and makes white clouds stand out boldly.

The UV or Skylight filter is used with daylight-type colour film. It helps to avoid unpleasant blue cast when the sun goes in, or when working in the shade (Agfa CT18, by the way, does not suffer from this fault). As no increase in exposure is required, this filter may be left in place at all times. It also helps protect the expensive surface of the lens itself.

The exposure meter, of course, eliminates guesswork, and gives a satisfactorily high level of good results.

Close-up accessories

The single-lens reflex camera has obvious advantages for extreme close-up work. The most important is that parallax (the different viewpoints of lens and viewfinder) does not exist. One sees exactly what one will get on the film. For this reason, close-up attachments for such cameras tend to be simpler (and cheaper) than for other camera systems.

The simplest close-up attachment is a close-up lens, placed over the camera lens in the same way as a filter. A close-up lens of one diopter will allow photography of, say, a cluster of blooms. A lens of 2 diopters will allow one to fill the frame with a single bloom, while a 3-diopter lens approaches closer still.

Similar lenses can be obtained in pairs for twin-lens reflex cameras, and often the lens covering the camera's viewing lens includes a wedge to compensate for the acute parallax gap.

Different optical devices perform the same function on rangefinder cameras.

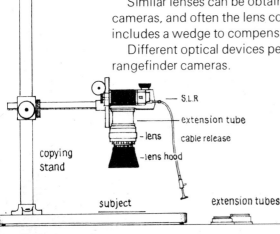

S.L.R

extension tube

– lens

cable release

copying stand

– lens hood

subject

extension tubes

Close-up lenses are all right for general work, but will not give the same optical performance (especially at the edge of the field) as when the camera lens is used in conjunction with extension tubes or bellows.

Extension tubes

Usually provided in sets of three, an extension tube is fitted between the camera body and the camera lens, thus providing an extension to the camera's focusing system. Certain tubes are available which will transmit the action of the SLR's automatic diaphragm mechanism. These are far better than non-automatic tubes for hand-held work, as focusing (very critical in close-up work) must be done at full aperture.

Close-up tubes may be used singly or in combination, and a set of three combined will allow the camera to be used at a distance of a few centimetres. Manufacturers supply a table of exposure increase factors for various combinations of tubes used in conjunction with lenses of various focal lengths.

extension tubes were used to copy this Victorian playbill. The camera (Praktica, 55mm) was supported on a stand (see opposite). Daylight, 1/5 second at f16, Kodachrome 11

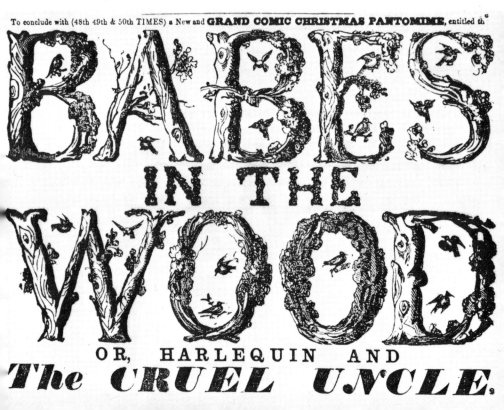

Slide copiers

This is a device which enables one to make duplicates of colour transparencies. The slide to be copied is held in a frame to which the camera is attached, and a 1 : 1 extension is provided. The more expensive slide copiers allow a certain amount of compositional correction by means of vertical and horizontal movements. Exposures are best made by electronic flash or blue bulbs, using daylight colour film in the camera. Once the correct exposure is found, a careful note should be taken of the flash-to-slide distance, so that identical exposures can be made in future.

Slide copying can also be done with bellows extensions.

Tripods

Some of the tripods available on the amateur market, even though they may carry the grandiose label 'pro', are almost useless for serious work.

The test of a good tripod is not simply to bear down on it with the palm of the hand, but to try twisting the top from side to side. Good tripods are best bought from the genuine professional ranges (Linhof, Gitzo, de Vere, etc.), normally advertised in the professional rather than the amateur photographic journals.

The tripod should be equipped with a large ball-and-socket or pan-tilt head.

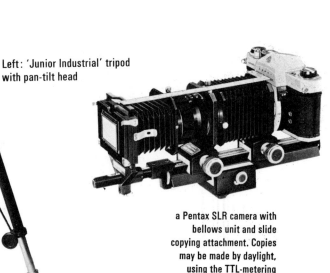

Left: 'Junior Industrial' tripod with pan-tilt head

a Pentax SLR camera with bellows unit and slide copying attachment. Copies may be made by daylight, using the TTL-metering system

6. Available light

Fast emulsions and high speed lenses make it possible to photograph the human scene at even the lowest light levels. 'Available light' is the phrase used to describe such photography. A more pat description might be 'available dark'.

The advocates of available light work make full use of wide aperture lenses and fast films, often 'pushing' these, by means of extended development, so that printable images may be obtained in circumstances which normally would suggest the use of flash.

Special high-speed film and developer combinations will be given in Chapter 8.

In this short chapter, it will be useful to sort out some of the muddled thinking that exists about this type of work.

Members of the 'old school' often scorn available light work in the same way that they scorn the miniature camera. Technical quality plays a large part in the kind of work they are interested in, composition follows a few conventional rules, and often the 'picture content', or subject matter, is chosen as a mere vehicle for a demonstration of technical competence.

At the other end of the scale, and no less partisan, are those to whom coarse grain has become a god, and for whom technical quality of any kind detracts from their purpose.

Between these two extremes are the large body of sensible photographers who put the picture first, but try to produce it with good technical quality.

What must be understood is that available light work makes its own demands on the photographer – and most of these demands are hardly compatible with quality in the sense understood by the 'old school'.

Equipment must be handy and ready for instant use. Some exponents almost invariably work with a wide-angle lens at full aperture, changing only the shutter speeds as necessary. The wide-angle ensures that the photographer will always be able to include the whole of his subject – too much if he has no time to approach close enough, but the relevant negative section may be enlarged later. The short focal length also gives reasonable depth of field, even at the large aperture used.

The user of available light puts the *picture first,* and neither seeks, nor worries about, the possible incidence of grain.

A few photographers, determined to be modern at all costs, try to copy the work of the leading practitioners of available light photography. Unfortunately, they see only the coarse grain, and not the picture content. From this they infer that the success of such work depends on producing the coarsest possible grain.

Advertising photographers frequently exaggerate grain structure to the point where line blocks can be made from half-tone prints. As a great deal of artistic know-how goes into the images behind the grain, such pictures are in a class by themselves – neither a mere exercise in the production of grain, nor a straightforward attempt at available light photography, though they often contain great artistic merit in their own right.

7. Using flash creatively

There are two kinds of flash lighting: bulb and electronic. Each has certain peculiarities. The photographer who requires just a few flashes from time to time would do better to buy a small bulb flashgun for about £2–£3. A handful of small bulbs weighs next to nothing, takes up very little space, but provides a considerable light output.

Those who require a large number of flashes at fairly frequent intervals will find it cheaper in the long run to buy electronic flash. Electronic flashguns work best if they are used frequently, and the cost per flash may be as low as a half pence. Against that of course, is the relatively high purchase price of the equipment.

Most flashbulbs are now provided with a blue coating, which makes them suitable for use with daylight-type colour film. Such bulbs are also suitable for use with black and white film, and the general photographer has no need to buy uncoated flashbulbs, except for some special purpose.

Modern electronic units emit a flash of approximately the same colour temperature as daylight, and are therefore suitable for use, unfiltered, with daylight-type colour, or black and white film.

We are concerned with two basic aspects of flash photography; the technical, and the aesthetic. To use flash competently, we should understand a few simple rules.

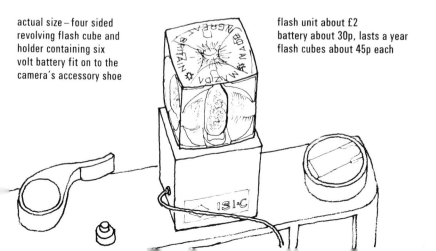

actual size – four sided revolving flash cube and holder containing six volt battery fit on to the camera's accessory shoe

flash unit about £2
battery about 30p, lasts a year
flash cubes about 45p each

this Japanese Minette
flashgun costs about
£3·50 and takes three
different types of bulb

this one-piece electronic
flash, the Sunpak Auto
Zoom 4000, has a remote
sensor attached to the
camera giving correct
exposure even when the
flash is pointed towards
the ceiling for bounce-flash
work. Cost: about £59

The light emitted by an electronic flash or by one particular kind of flashbulb will always be of the same power, barring mechanical faults, and so it becomes quite simple to estimate exposure accurately.

DIN ASA	1.5m 5 ft	2 m 7 ft	3 m 10 ft	4 m 13 ft	5 m 16 ft
15-17 25-40	11	8	5,6	4	2,8
19-20 50-80	16	11	8	5,6	4
21-23 100-160	22	16	11	8	5,6

In general, the packet containing flashbulbs carries a table, showing the correct lens apertures to use at different distances, with films of various ASA ratings. Every modern electronic flashgun incorporates a disc calculator. Having set the ASA rating of the film, the disc is turned until the distance setting meets a pointer. The correct lens aperture may then be read off, and set on the camera lens.

Guide numbers

For more advanced work, the photographer makes use of a *guide number,* provided by the manufacturer of the flashbulb or electronic unit. One simply divides the guide number by the distance and the answer is the correct aperture to use. Guide numbers are usually given in both feet and metres.

For example, the tiny AG1B (the B stands for Blue) flashbulb has a guide number of 55, in feet, when used with the relatively slow Kodachrome film, daylight-type. If we want to take a portrait at 5 ft distance:

$$55 \div 5 = f11$$

Guide numbers are as simple as that. If one needs to ascertain the guide number of a particular electronic outfit for a particular film, one merely sets the calculator for the ASA rating of the film, then multiplies any of the distances by the f number opposite. If, for example, the calculator of a small electronic unit, set for a film of 50 ASA, reads $f11$ at 4 ft, the guide number is 44. The same setting will also read $f8$ at about 6 ft, or $f4$ at 11 ft, any of which multiplications will give the same guide number.

Do not fall into the type of thinking that at twice the distance one opens the lens by one stop. The intensity of light falls off in inverse ratio to the square of the distance. Thus, at twice the distance one needs to give four times the exposure, i.e. one opens the lens *two* stops.

Flash on camera

Most flashguns are provided with a very short trigger lead (connecting the flash outfit to the synchronizing socket of the camera). This is adequate when the flash is used on the camera, clipped into a shoe or attached to a bracket, but used this way, the quality of the flash lighting is strictly utilitarian in character. It comes from dead in front, and provides no modelling.

The quality of the light becomes much more interesting if the flash is removed from the camera. A 1m extension lead from the flash outfit, allows the photographer to hold the flash away from the camera and position it at a variety of angles. An even longer extension lead, say 3.7m in length, allows the flash to be placed on some convenient support while the photographer moves around freely at the other end of the lead.

Extension leads are particularly useful when practising bounce flash.

Bounce flash

This is the most popular method of using flash among professionals. Instead of being directed at the subject, the flash is aimed at the ceiling or at some other convenient reflecting surface, such as a light-toned wall.

Such lighting simulates normal room lighting, but the pictures are characterized by extreme sharpness and depth of field.

bounce flash allows lively pictures indoors as in this shot of film star Barbara Bouchet. Taken on High Speed Ektachrome Daylight Type and a Sunpak electronic flash aimed at the ceiling

Naturally, more exposure is required than when the flash is aimed direct at the subject, as the light is more diffused and has farther to travel.

Three variables exist: the distance from flash to reflective surface, the tone of the reflective surface, and the distance from the reflective surface to the subject. In average rooms, it is generally recommended to open the lens two stops wider than would be required if the flash were used direct from a distance of 2.7m. This is irrespective of the actual distance from which the bounce flash exposure is to be made.

Owing to the extra exposure needed, bounce flash with small electronic units is not always possible when very slow films are used. Here is a simple method of ascertaining correct bounce flash exposure with any particular flash source.

Load the camera with fast film and go into any room with which you are familiar, and to which

you have constant access. It need conform to no specification other than moderately light-toned ceiling and walls. This will be *your* average room.

Place a model about 2.7m in front of you, and not closer than 1m to a wall. Point the flash at the ceiling midway between you and the model (the actual angle is not critical). Hold the flash high, so that no direct light spills on to the model.

Now make a series of exposures, using every lens stop from the largest to the smallest.

After developing the film, choose the negative that prints most easily. You have now established the correct aperture to use in your average room.

Computer flashguns measure the flash reflected from the subject and terminate the exposure when enough has been given. Computer flash with a remote sensor (see page 62) can also be used for bounce-flash pictures. Used for either direct or bounce-flash, they eliminate the need to work out apertures from guide numbers.

bounced flash gives the most natural effect. Here the ceiling was the main reflector

Multiple flash

Professional bulb or electronic units have provision for plugging in an extension flash head, so that two light sources may be used.

If such provision is not made, a second flash unit may be fired in synchronization with the first unit, by means of what is called a slave unit.

The first unit is connected to the camera in the usual way. The second unit is placed where required, and the slave unit attached to its trigger lead. The cell portion of the slave unit is pointed towards the flash unit which is connected to the camera.

When the first flash fires, the slave unit picks up the light impulse and fires the unit to which it is attached. There is no time-lag between the two flashes.

The flash connected to the camera usually provides fill-in illumination to lighten the shadows cast by the extension light, which is used as a 'modeller'.

Several extensions or slave units may be used to provide more complicated lighting effects.

It should be remembered that when two lamps of equal power are used from the same position, the exposure required will be 1·4 times less than for one bulb.

Also, if the second bulb is positioned at an angle of more than 60° from the axis between the first bulb and the subject, exposure should be calculated *only* for the first bulb.

an electronic flashgun is being used on a dull day to simulate low evening sunlight

Synchron-ization

When an electronic unit is triggered, the flash immediately reaches its peak intensity, lasts for a mere 1/500th or 1/1000th of a second, and dies.

A flashbulb, filled with hydrolanium wire, is ignited from the filament at its centre, and burns outward. The intensity of the light increases up to a peak, levels out on a 'plateau', then dies away.

Whereas the electronic flash immediately reaches its peak, the flashbulb takes perhaps 20 milliseconds to do so. This is why modern camera shutters are fitted with two separate flash sockets, marked X and M, or X and FP. The X contact triggers the flash immediately the shutter is released. The M and FP contacts provide a short synchronizing delay while the bulb is reaching its peak illumination.

This latter setting is only necessary where a higher shutter speed is used than the total effective speed of the flashbulb (about 1/30th second with M-class bulbs). On the packets used for flashbulbs will be found reduced guide numbers for use when higher shutter speeds are in use.

Front-lens shutters may be used at all shutter speeds with flashbulbs and electronic flash, provided the M socket is used for the former, and the X socket for the latter.

Synchronization of focal plane shutters provides certain problems that do not exist with front-lens shutters. This is due to the time it takes for the slit in the focal plane blind to traverse the film plane. Normally, the small focal plane shutter must not be set at a faster speed than 1/50th second when an electronic flash is used (X setting), or 1/15th second when using M-class flashbulbs (still on the X setting). Use of faster shutter speeds will result in uneven or part exposure of the negative.

A special type of flashbulb (FP, for focal plane) is obtainable. This has a special long peak, and will give even illumination on focal plane shutters at all speeds (FP setting).

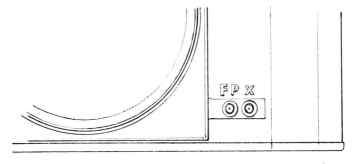

Fill-in flash

Sometimes called synchro-sunlight, this method is used to relieve dense shadows cast by the sun. The prime exposure is set by using the exposure meter, and the flash simply lightens the shadows without appreciably affecting the all-over exposure.

The usual procedure is to control the flash so that it gives one stop under-exposure in relation to the normal guide number or calculator. This will raise the light-level in the shadows to a ratio of 1 : 4 with the sunlit highlights of the subject.

This is because outdoors, where there are no reflective surfaces, the flash will be about half as effective as when used indoors. If we then use one stop smaller than suggested by the calculator or guide number we will be two stops under-exposed.

Suppose we are photographing a girl on a sunny beach and the correct exposure is 1/250th at f8. We are 3m from our subject. Our normal flash guide number, we shall say, is 80 for the film in use. Dividing the guide number by the distance gives us an aperture of f8, the same as we are using for our sunlight exposure.

As we are outdoors the *effective* flash exposure at f8 will give us a shadow-highlight ratio of 1 : 2. This would put too much light into the shadows. What we need to do is halve the power

Normal daylight without flash fill-in.

too much flash fill-in kills all modelling

one small flash unit held close to the rear-left and high, simulates sunshine. Here, the daylight is, in effect providing the fill-in illumination.

of the flash. This is easily done by placing a paper tissue, or thin white handkerchief, over the flash reflector, or even by removing the reflector itself.

The same effect can also be achieved by removing the flash (not the camera) farther from the subject by means of an extension lead. This, of course, means that an assistant must be used to hold the flash.

The creative light

Do not look upon flash as a utility light, only to be used in emergencies – though it is, of course, very good for that purpose.

Use it with as much imagination as though you were arranging photofloods. When using bounce flash, do not slavishly use the ceiling every time. Try bouncing the light from a wall (giving the same exposure). This provides an interesting side light, but there will be sufficient light reflecting back again from the other side of the room to fill in the shadows nicely.

Even a single flash aimed at the subject will produce far better modelling when used off the camera as suggested.

If you have a bulb flashgun with a collapsible reflector, try exposing with the bare flashbulb, minus reflector. At middle distance (say between 3–4.6m) this gives a combination of direct and bounce flash. The lamp should always be used to one side, and preferably high, when using this technique. Exposure increase will normally be about one stop.

the white cloth reduces the light by half and helps to avoid an artificial effect when flash is a secondary source of light

8. Processing the film

The majority of amateur photographers take their rolls of exposed film to the local chemist for developing and printing, but when you become more expert and when you have got to the stage of experimenting with different effects, it is much more satisfactory to do your own developing, printing, and enlarging, none of which is particularly difficult.

The first essential is to have a clear knowledge of the nature of the actual film. If we were to take it from the camera and examine it in the light we would see that it is coated with a creamy surface. This is the emulsion, basically a binder of gelatin holding in suspension thousands of tiny grains of silver halides.

Silver halide is the light-sensitive agent. It is formed by combining silver with members of the group called halogens — bromine, chlorine, and iodine.

When the film inside the dark body of the camera was exposed, the lens threw a 'light image' of the view before it on to the film, and the silver halides were 'burnt' by the action of the light.

This 'burnt' image, not yet visible, is called the latent image, and can be revealed by using a developer.

Where a bright light (say, a sky) fell on the film, the silver halides were strongly affected and will blacken during development. Where the image of a dark object, or shadow area, fell on the film, the silver halides were only lightly affected and will later be dissolved away by the action of the fixer, leaving the emulsion clear, or nearly so. Thus, the negative is a reversal of the tones of the original scene, hence its name.

All the developer does is blacken the affected silver halides, so that they become a visible image.

After development, still in the dark, the film is treated in an acid stop bath. This does two things. It removes excess developer still clinging to the emulsion, and at the same time neutralizes the still active developer carried over in the emulsion. This latter action effectively stops development, whereas a plain water rinse merely slows development.

A fixer-hardener is then used. The fixer removes the unexposed silver halides from the emulsion, leaving only the visible, developed image. It also removes the remaining sensitivity of the film and after this stage we can work in full room lighting. The hardener protects the emulsion from abrasion both during its wet period and later.

Finally, the film is washed to remove the fixer after it has done its job.

The most universal of all film developers is the Kodak formula D 76 (Ilford ID 11, May & Baker 320). D 76 utilizes the full speed of the film, gives relatively fine grain and good sharpness and is the standard developer by which all others are judged. It can be purchased in powder form in packs to make 600ml and should be made up according to the maker's directions.

Proprietary stop bath may be bought in packets, but it is quite simple, and much cheaper, to make up for oneself. 15ml of 80% acetic acid is stirred into 300ml of water, and the total volume then increased to 600ml with water.

Concentrated liquid fixers, and fixing salts, are marketed by all manufacturers of photographic chemicals and are made up according to the maker's directions. The purchaser should make sure that they contain a hardening agent.

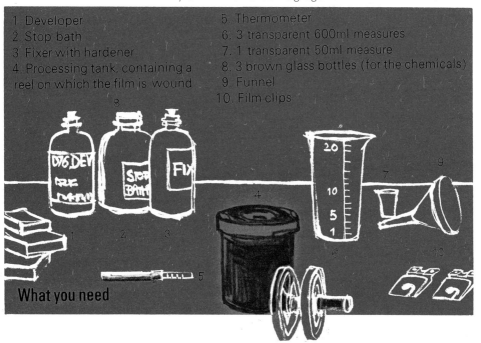

1. Developer
2. Stop bath
3. Fixer with hardener
4. Processing tank, containing a reel on which the film is wound
5. Thermometer
6. 3 transparent 600ml measures
7. 1 transparent 50ml measure
8. 3 brown glass bottles (for the chemicals)
9. Funnel
10. Film clips

What you need

Step One   In complete darkness the film is loaded into the tank. When you buy a tank insist on a demonstration of how a film is loaded into it. The action is quite simple, and is quickly mastered when once seen.

After the tank lid is secured, the remaining steps can be carried out with the light on.

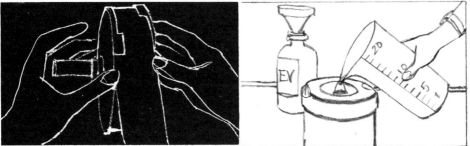

Step Two   The developer, stop bath, and fixer have been poured out in the right amounts (usually 300ml for 35mm films, and 450ml with 120-size films. Actual amounts depend on the make of tank).

All three solutions are brought to 68 °F. (20 °C.). The tank is tilted slightly, to avoid air traps, and the developer poured quickly and smoothly through the light-trapped entry port in the tank lid.

The film is agitated inside the tank (various means are provided) for the first five seconds and thereafter for five seconds at minute intervals, until development is complete.

Here are developing times for a number of popular films developed in D 76 at 68 °F. (20 °C.):

35mm film		min	120 film		min
Tri-X	(400ASA)	7	Tri-X	(400ASA)	8
HP4	(400ASA)	7½	HP4	(400ASA)	9
Agfapan 400	(400ASA)	8	Agfapan 400	(400ASA)	9½
Plus-X	(125ASA)	6	Plus-X	(125ASA)	6
FP4	(125ASA)	6	FP4	(125ASA)	6
Agfapan 100	(100ASA)	6	Agfapan 100	(100ASA)	7
Pan F	(50ASA)	6	Isopan IF	(40ASA)	6½
Pan-X	(32ASA)	5½	Pan-X	(32ASA)	7
Agfapan 25	(25ASA)	5½	Agfapan 25	(25ASA)	6

high speed films	Special high speed films in special developers: Agfapan 1000, 35mm and 120 (1000 ASA) using Rodinal developer diluted 1 : 50. 18 minutes. Kodak Royal-X, 120 size, developed in Kodak DK-50, with 5 seconds' agitation per minute. 9 minutes. This gives an ASA rating of 1250. With flatly-lit subjects the ASA rating may be raised to 2000 and development extended to 12 minutes (continuous agitation).

Step Three

Fifteen or twenty seconds before development is complete, pour the developer from the tank into its bottle. Immediately, pour the stop bath into the tank and agitate for half a minute. Pour the stop bath back into its bottle.

Step Four

Pour the fixer-hardener into the tank. Agitate occasionally during the fixing period recommended for the particular solution in use. Rapid fixers such as 'Amfix' complete the job in a fraction of the time, contain an excellent hardener, and wash out of the film more easily than common fixing salt. Pour the fixer-hardener back into its bottle.

Step Five

Wash the film for ten to fifteen minutes under running water. This may be accomplished with the lid on or off the tank. In cold weather use a jug to lower the temperature of the water by 15°C. steps at half-minute intervals until the temperature of the tap water is reached. This avoids damage to the still soft emulsion, which may result in an ugly reticulated pattern.

Step Six

Put a film clip at the top and bottom of the film and hang up to dry in a dust-free atmosphere. Some workers wipe the film down carefully with a wrung-out chamois leather, or squeegee it once between the rubber blades of a film wiper. Others prefer to introduce a few drops of wetting agent to the final wash water and hang up without wiping. The wetting agent avoids white drying marks caused by hard water.

That is all, except that the dried film should be cut into strips of five or six (35mm) or three or four (120), and filed in clean film wallets. These consist of transparent sleeves inside a paper wallet, each of which accommodates a complete film.

The ideal negative

There is really no such thing. Some of the most successful pictures ever taken were printed from over- or under-exposed negatives with unsharp images, incorrectly developed.

At the same time, one can describe a technically ideal negative, for teaching purposes.

This should contain a full range of tones and should produce its best print on a **normal** grade of printing paper. When the perfect negative is pressed in contact with a sheet of newspaper in a good light, the print should be just visible through the darkest parts of the negative.

<u>correctly exposed neg</u>.
good tonal range with
no extremes of contrast

print on normal paper gives
good balance of tone overall

lively colour

detail held in shadows

light tones he

good modelling and colour in
face & eyes

← under exposed neg.
detail lost in shadows

over exposed neg.
↓ too dark — highlights dense

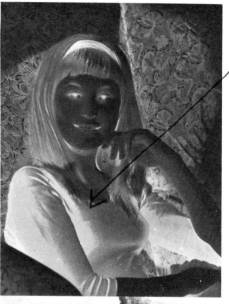

shadow detail hard to print

↑ print on normal paper is
too low in key for the subject.
shadows dull & dark, skin-
tones incorrect and under-
... Print on hard paper
would help if carefully
...ined.

Face lacks
modelling

composition spoilt by
jumpy tones

tone & detail lost

try
soft
paper

9. Printing and enlarging

a 35mm contact print is usually big enough to show you where you went wrong

The photographer who uses a large film size has one advantage over his colleague who uses 35mm. He may fill an album with 6 × 6cm pictures, which are large enough for normal viewing, and make enlargements from the few which are worth it.

A 35mm contact print, while quite large enough for identification purposes, is too small to be considered as a picture in its own right. This may or may not be considered a disadvantage. On the other hand, because of the cost of large sheets of printing paper, some 35mm negatives do not get enlarged, though they deserve it. On the other hand, the 35mm user learns to be very selective, both at the taking stage, and while selecting negatives for enlargement.

This may be done either in subdued room lighting or in the dark-room. In the former case, one uses contact printing paper (such as Kodak Velox), in the latter bromide or chloro-bromide paper as used for enlargements.

In either case, the paper is laid emulsion side up, and the negative, emulsion side down, is pressed into contact with it by means of a sheet of glass. Small printing frames are obtainable, which will accommodate a single 6 × 6cm negative, together with a border mask, but this is a very slow process. It is far quicker to contact a whole film on one sheet of paper.

A single sheet of 20.3 × 25.4cm paper will take one 120-size film (three strips of four negatives, or four strips of three), or one 36-exposure 35mm film (six strips of six).

A useful device, which enhances the appearance of the finished sheet, is the Paterson contact proof printer. All negatives are held simply and neatly in parallel rows, with negative numbers visible beneath each frame. A data panel is printed automatically along one edge of the print.

Contact sheets made this way fit neatly into a special filing system, which provides ready access to any negative and its related contact print.

To contact print by room lighting, work in the shadow of

your body at the far side of the room from the light. Expose the contact paper to the light as little as possible before the actual exposure is made, or the print will show grey fogging.

Place the negative, or negatives, in position in the frame, swiftly remove a sheet of paper from its packet, place in contact with the negatives (emulsion to emulsion) and close the frame. Make sure the packet of paper is closed at once.

The paper is then exposed to a light. An exposure of 2—8 seconds at 1.8m from a 40-watt bulb should be suitable, though actual exposure will be found by trial.

Development may then take place in very subdued light. The print should stay face down in the developer, but may be turned up occasionally for a quick glance.

When making contact prints on bromide paper in the dark-room using the enlarger, the printing frame is placed face upwards on the enlarger baseboard, and the enlarger head raised to the top of the column. With an empty negative carrier, the exposure is made with the lens stopped down one or two stops. A few trials will establish the correct exposure time.

In spite of the fact that bromide paper is more sensitive than contact printing paper, in the dark-room one works comfortably by the light of a safe light. Some workers do not use a special frame, merely laying the paper emulsion side up on the baseboard, arranging the negative face downwards on the paper, then laying a clean sheet of fairly heavy glass on top. This is not so neat, and one must make sure that the two emulsions are firmly in contact at all points.

The paper is then developed normally.

The enlarger

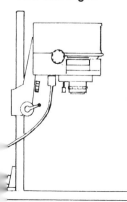

If you are proposing to do all your own processing, you will certainly need an enlarger, of which there are many good examples on the market, ranging from £30 to over £200.

To obtain vibration-free enlargement, the top of the enlarger column should be braced against a small block of wood or rubber attached to the wall. Especially when the enlarger head is raised for really big enlargements, this ensures that fine detail will not be lost.

Glassless negative carriers are often preferred, as there are then less surfaces to pick up dust and hairs, which cause white spots on the prints. However, after a negative warms up in the enlarger it sometimes buckles. A similar thing happens with

card-mounted transparencies when placed in a warm projecto
The transparency 'pops', and the image on the screen must be refocused.

Even if the negative in the enlarger is refocused after buckling, the curvature means that really sharp focus cannot be obtained at all points of the print. For this reason, a means of holding the negative flat should be used when the highest technical quality is sought.

The most general way, is to use a glass negative carrier, and to take special care to see that all surfaces are dust-free. The best possible way is to use an enlarger incorporating a design where the condenser itself presses the negative flat across an opening in a simple metal carrier. This design is incorporated in Leitz, Reid, and Gamer enlargers. An adjustable paper holder is required, to hold the printing paper.

paper holder

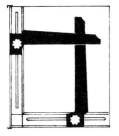

A suitable grade of paper

One normally speaks of negatives as being of soft, normal, or contrasty quality. A technician might refer to these as being of short, medium, or steep gradation. The characteristic appearance of three such negatives can be seen in the illustration (pages 74–75).

Whereas the contrast of a negative may be controlled by shortening or lengthening the development time, printing papers will give a satisfactory image tone only when fully developed. Prints of good gradation from negatives of widely differing contrast can therefore be made only by selecting a grade of paper suitable to a particular range of densities.

Thus, to obtain conventional print quality, a negative of normal contrast is printed on a normal grade of paper. A soft negative is compensated for by the use of a contrasty, or hard, grade of paper. A contrasty negative is printed on a soft grade of paper.

Although most paper manufacturers provide up to five or s
grades of paper, from very soft to extremely contrasty, the beginner is advised to practise with only three grades of pape
soft, normal, and hard. These should be in a glossy surface. Th
provides more information about a paper's tone-producing qualities than does an art-surfaced paper. 20.3 × 25.4cm is a suitable size for practice, being easily handled, but large enou
to reveal quality differences between various films and developers.

The dark-room

Whether this is a special room or a large rubber-covered board over the bath is merely a matter of convenience. The highest quality work may be produced in a cupboard under the stairs provided care is taken.

Apart from the enlarger and a supply of printing paper, one requires:

Paper developer (see maker's recommendation).
Stop bath (the same one used for negatives will do).
Fixer (usually more dilute than for film: see maker's recommendations).
Three 25.4 × 30.4cm dishes (easier to handle 20.3 × 25.4cm paper in these).
1 safe light (see recommendations of paper manufacturer).
1 large washing-up bowl (if sink not available).

The dishes should be arranged in sequence, so that the paper is taken from enlarger to developer, then stop bath, then fixer, then washing-up bowl or sink.

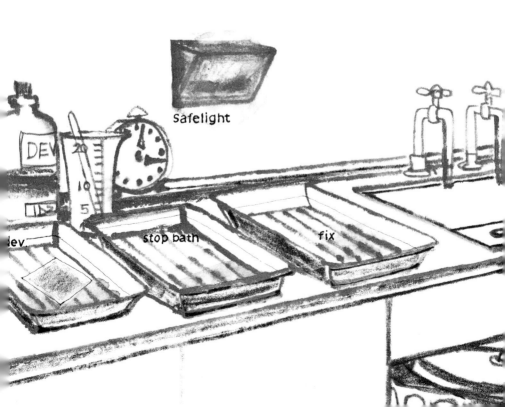

safelight

dev

stop bath

fix

The method

In a modern enlarger, where a condenser is used in conjunction with an opal lamp, printing times for normal negatives are quite short. With the enlarging lens stopped down about two stops, a 20.3 × 25.4cm print should be properly exposed at ten seconds. This will vary a good deal with negative density, the enlarger lens, the power of the enlarger lamp and so on, but it does provide a basis for experiment.

1. Put the negative in the carrier, switch on the enlarger light, and raise the head of the enlarger until the projected image is approximately of the desired size. Now bring the image into sharp focus by adjusting the lens. Stop the lens down two stops and switch off the enlarger.

The safe-light should be at distance that will allow one to work the various controls, but not close enough to interfere with viewing of the image.

2. For an apparently normal negative, place a sheet of normal grade paper in the paper holder, surface upwards. Switch on the enlarger for ten seconds, or whatever your trial period is to be. Switch off.

3. Slide the paper under the developer with an even motion, to avoid air bubbles and uneven development. Turn the paper face downwards and rock the dish gently. Keep the paper face downwards for the first half minute. This is when the paper is still most sensitive, and there is nothing to see anyway.

After half a minute the print may be turned face up while the developing image appears. Some paper manufacturers recommend $1\frac{1}{2}$–2 minutes for full development. The golden rule is: *develop for two full minutes* even if the image is getting much too dark. In this way, one eliminates one of the most troublesome variables. We shall see why in a moment.

Drip off the print, immerse for a few seconds in the stop bath, then transfer to the fixer. Rock the dish to ensure that the print is completely covered by solution. Repeat at half-minute intervals. If rapid fixer is used, the room lighting may be switched on after fifteen or twenty seconds, and fixation will be complete in five minutes. If normal fixing salt is used, room lighting may be switched on after half a minute, but full fixation will take ten minutes.

(a) If the fully developed print is too dark, expose another sheet of paper for less time.

(b) If the fully developed print is too light, expose another sheet of paper for more time.

Having obtained the best possible print:

(c) If this is too contrasty, print on a softer grade of paper. If necessary repeat (a) or (b).

(d) If this is too soft, print on a harder grade of paper. If necessary repeat (a) or (b).

4. After fixing is complete, drip off the print and transfer to the sink (or via the washing-up bowl to the kitchen sink), and wash thoroughly. The prints may be kept moving in a dish under running water for half an hour, or rocked in six or seven changes of clean water at five-minute intervals.

Rinse and dry hands every time developer or fixer is touched.

5. The prints are now dried. Special fluffless blotting paper, or blotting rolls, may be used to remove surplus moisture, and prints on doubleweight paper may then be hung to dry by one corner. This is not satisfactory with singleweight prints, as these have a tendency to curl.

The best method of drying either weight is in a drying press. Art surfaced prints are placed face upwards in the hot dryer and a tensioned apron lowered over them. Full drying takes just a few minutes.

Glossy prints may be squeegeed on to chromium or stainless steel glazing plates, which are put in the dryer in the same way. This produces a highly glazed surface to the print.

Spotting

If, in spite of your efforts to keep the negative and carrier clean, a white spot or a hairline appears on the print, it can be spotted out.

Use a tiny drop of Martin's Retouching Dye (black), produced by Philadelphus Jeyes & Co Ltd of 6 The Drapery, Northampton. Most professionals do.

The merest spot is taken up on a damp brush, which is then wiped almost dry. The white spot is touched once or twice, until the required density has built up. The dye is invisible on the print. If applied to a glossy print while still damp, the print may then be glazed over.

print
dryer

10. Portraits are for personality

A person's face in repose is like a map. It may show the contours, but not necessarily the character underneath.

Formal portraiture, calling as it does for great care with lighting and posing, and relatively slow exposure, tends to treat the face as a map. At best, a smile is introduced.

Modern small cameras with fast lenses and fast film allow the photographer to reveal the true character beneath the surface. Sitters may speak, and be spoken to. The clever portraitist is a conversationalist, too. He coaxes from his sitter whatever responses – gaiety, wistfulness, thoughtfulness, and so on – best portray the sitter's character.

The very last phrase one should use in modern portrait work, is 'Hold it!'

For this kind of portraiture lighting is arranged to give generally pleasing contours, but strong modelling lights should be avoided. The sudden movement of a head, as in a laugh, will send a carefully-arranged, sharply-outlined nose shadow racing across the cheek. Diffused or reflected light, especially bounced flash, will produce far better results.

When photographing a lively sitter it is best not to use a tripod. Sit facing the sitter, get him in focus, and observe him steadily in the viewfinder, talking to him at the same time. If the sitter leans backwards or forwards, do the same. This avoids the necessity for rapidly refocusing the lens.

With female sitters the fine skin tone can be retained by using a medium speed, instead of a fast film. Photoflood bulbs, even when diffused, will provide enough light for the camera to be hand-held. For the more pensive pose, of course, a tripod can be used.

As suggested in Chapter 7, a flash unit may be used at the end of a long extension trigger lead. For portraiture, the flash unit should be placed very much to one side, and aimed at ceiling or wall to provide better modelling.

a 6cm-square snapshot exploits the soft lighting conditions which can occur at the seaside. There is plenty of light but none of the pitfalls of strong sun and shadow. Courtesy of Ilford Limited

Formal lighting

Formal portrait lighting is built up according to a logical pattern. First, a *modelling* lamp is positioned to show the bone structure and features to their best advantage. This is usually at 45° from the camera, and at least 45° high. A less powerful and more diffused light is used close to the camera. This is called a *fill-in*, and serves the purpose of lightening the heavy shadows cast by the *modeller*.

A third lamp, called a *background* lamp, is to the side of the sitter, and aimed at the background. It serves the purpose of separating the sitter from the background. Sometimes, one *background* lamp is used from each side.

An *effect* lamp, usually a narrow-beam spot, is placed to the side and rear of the sitter, and is directed at the sitter's face or hair, giving a rim light to the former and/or a sheen to the latter.

Success in formal portraiture calls for a large space to work in, as small rooms do not give the necessary space *behind* the sitter. Two or three large paper backgrounds (white, grey, and black for black and white work, or pastel shades for colour) help one achieve professional results. These may be had in 2m or 3m rolls, and suspended from special poles.

Two or three floods and one or two spots on good extensible stands (one spot on a boom) mean a sizeable outlay in hard cash, so don't start buying until you are quite sure that you really want to specialize in portraiture.

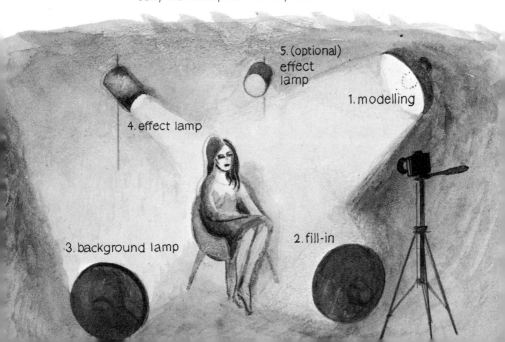

5. (optional) effect lamp

1. modelling

4. effect lamp

3. background lamp

2. fill-in

this portrait simply uses two lights: a spotlight from behind the profile and a floodlight in front. By Wolf Wehran, Zeiss Contarex, 85mm Sonnar (FP4 film)

11. Vision and composition

The title of this chapter is really two titles: 'Vision' and 'Composition'. Academic study of the work of great artists throughout the centuries has given rise to a set of formal rules of composition. These are useful in teaching students to arrange the elements of their pictures harmoniously. Such rules, however, cannot teach the student how to *see* a picture

The right way is to look at anything and everything, noticing shapes, the juxtaposition of masses, of light and shade, harmonies and discords, restful or active relationships, unusual or formal combinations, the mood of colour, of light and texture. The subject itself is far less important than the way it is seen and photographed.

As an aid to the development of vision, let us study a few of the rules of composition, especially as these apply to the photographic medium:

1. Simplicity pays. A great deal of detail spread over the picture space can be very distracting. Large, plain masses of balancing tones are more satisfying.
2. Avoid horizontal or vertical lines cutting the picture into two halves. Horizon lines should be above or below centre. If good clouds are present, two-thirds sky gives a sound result.
3. Keep subjects of strong interest away from margins and corners.
4. Wherever possible, choose a viewpoint that places the highest light against the strongest shadow.
5. In an 'ideal' composition, the eye is led from the main point of interest, across the centre of the picture, and comes to rest on a correlated interest at the other side. It is balance we require, not symmetry.
6. A bad composition is one where the eye finds no opposing balance of lines and tones, and is led to the margin of the picture
7. If figures are included, these should be facing or moving into the picture space, not out of it.

Like all rules, these are meant to be broken — but only after one has learned to apply them.

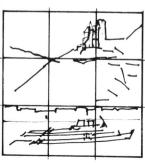

the main lines of this composition tend to divide the square into vertical and horizontal thirds. Agfacolor 6 × 6 cm taken on the River Rhine by Dr Johannes Zachs

Snapshots, as distinct from well-organized pictures, almost invariably contain a great deal of background detail — clothes lines, windows and flower beds, passers-by, and a hundred and one other objects. At the moment of taking his photograph, the photographer saw only his subject and forgot that the camera would record everything within its field of view. This background detail provides distraction from the main subject matter.

Thus, careful choice of background will emphasize the subject. We give strength to the subject by isolating it. Simplicity is best for backgrounds.

Choosing a low viewpoint, or placing the subject on a high point, will isolate the subject against the sky. If the horizon is cluttered with trees, chimneys, buildings and spires, a very high viewpoint will isolate the subject against the plainer pattern of grass or pavement.

It is worth remembering that a detail may be more effective than the whole. The village pump, shown very large and forming a frame for part of the village street, may be more effective than a general view of the street. So may a close-up of one interesting inn sign.

Remember, also, that isolation can be achieved by the use of slow films in conjunction with large lens apertures. Bitty backgrounds can be thrown so far out of focus that they no longer form a distraction.

opposite: low and high viewpoints help to simplify backgrounds and create unusual compositions even with the stock material of the holiday snapshot

When working in colour, a new set of compositional 'rules' impose themselves upon those for black and white photography, although the latter still apply.

The very limitations of black and white film are often a strong point in its favour. Black and white enables the photographer to work with a colourless abstract of the scene before him. Colours do not interfere with light and shade values.

On the other hand, certain subjects are immeasurably better when treated in colour. Although, in black and white work, we accept a medium grey tone as representing a blue sky, a few streaks of grey are not so easily accepted as a representation of a sunset. This is because we *know* the sky is blue, but we do not know the particular combinations of colours in any given sunset.

Where we have control over what colours we will include in our pictures, the following tips will be found useful.

1. Only a few colours in one picture. Variegated flower beds are an awful subject for colour photography.

2. Light, pastel tones, with a single, strong dash of complementary colour, are more pleasing than bright, garish colours.

3. Fairly large, balancing areas of colour convey clarity. A hotch-potch of fussy colour detail is restless, and prevents harmony.

4. There can be colour only where there is light. Avoid large, dark areas, unless these are background to a good clear colour.

5. Avoid unsharpness, particularly in foreground objects. A background may be unsharp provided its colours are quiet.

6. Warm colours – red and yellow – belong in the foreground. Blues and greens are background colours. Wherever the subject permits, observation of this sequence will give plasticity and depth to your pictures.

7. When their proportions are equal, complementary colours are antagonistic. If one is prominent, the other subordinate, striking effects may be obtained.

shaded light gives unity to a scene which might have been a raucous medley of colour. But the picture is spoilt by self-conscious poses

12. Hobby and profession

For millions of desk-bound people photography is an ideal hobby. Camera clubs and photographic societies provide lectures, slide shows, competitions, exhibitions, portrait sessions and a platform for the exchange of ideas and techniques.

Information on local clubs can be obtained from Mr. A. L. Kennedy, B.Sc., Honorary Secretary, The Photographic Alliance of Great Britain, 267 Victoria Avenue, Ockbrook, Derby.

Professional photography

One should not assume that a 'professional' is, by definition, a better photographer than an 'amateur'.

'Professional' merely means that the photographer makes a living with his camera.

Due to the work of the Institute of Incorporated Photographers in offering a full teaching syllabus and a degree, the status of the professional photographer has now been brought into line with that of other professional men.

Anyone who seriously considers photography as a career should consult, right at the outset:

The Secretary, The Institute of Incorporated Photographers, Amwell End, Ware, Hertfordshire

Let us now take a look at the various branches of professional photography, and the methods of entry.

Advertising

The advertising photographer must be highly skilled in a number of special techniques, must possess very considerable flair and must also be a business man.

All of today's top names in advertising photography have reached their position by way of a number of jobs as assistants to other photographers, arranging lights, props and backgrounds under supervision, loading and changing dark slides and films, learning to process and enlarge, running errands, *and watching like a hawk the methods of the great man.*

Baby
The usual routine is to note all new arrivals in the birth columns of local and national newspapers. The parents are written to after five months, when most parents begin to think in terms of professional baby pictures and the work can be undertaken in the home or studio.

Commercial
Commercial photography proper calls for a thorough basic training in the use of the technical camera, with its many movements and applications. A fully equipped commercial studio contains everything necessary to produce a great variety of effects. Commercial photography also includes location assignments where a high degree of technical control over materials is necessary.

Fashion
This is perhaps the only field in which artistic flair is vastly more important than technical ability, and several top men have graduated to their positions via art school.

Industrial
Industrial photography differs from commercial only in so far as more location work is involved. An extremely interesting field, often calling for photo-journalistic approach, as when the sequence of a particular industrial process must be recorded.

Medical
Normal educational qualifications, such as four GCE 'O' level subjects, are usually called for, including a science subject, though this is not always the case. Additionally, the Institute of Incorporated Photographers Preliminary, or City and Guilds Intermediate Certificate in Photography, may be required.

Portrait
One enters this field usually via a junior post with a studio portraitist. Few studios exist today solely for portraiture, except in theatrical and variety work.

Press
There is some confusion between the terms 'press photography' and 'photo-journalism'. The division should really be between photography for newspapers which require one, or two, pictures to cover a current event, and magazines and supplements where a story can be treated in greater depth.

Many national figures in this field started work on local newspapers.
Those contemplating press work should seek advice from:
The Education and Research Officer, The National Union of Journalists, 314 Grays Inn Road, London W.C.1

a wideangle lens enables the photographer to look down on the subject and cut out unwanted background. Even at a wide aperture there is still sufficient depth of field. Kodachrome II in dull light, 1/60 second at *f*2.8 with a 28mm lens

Index